To Walk in The Spirit

Vicky Wilkinson

ISBN: 978-1-78364-347-9

www.obt.org.uk

****

The Open Bible Trust
Fordland Mount, Upper Basildon,
Reading, RG8 8LU, UK.

To Walk in The Spirit

Contents

Preface

Preface

Romans 8 is a Bible chapter that gives prominence to a contrast between a walk in the flesh and a walk in the Spirit. Verse 1, of the *NKJV* (see also verse 4) makes the statement that those who are in Christ Jesus do *not* walk according to the flesh but rather according to the Spirit. What does it mean to walk in the flesh? And what does it mean to walk in the Spirit?

The word "flesh" *(KJV; NKJV)* is translated from the Greek word *sarx* and can mean the flesh of a human or animal, human nature with all its frailties, or a symbol of that which is external. The *NIV* chooses to translate *sarx* as "sinful nature". Therefore, when Romans 8:5 speaks of living "according to the flesh", it means to conduct our daily lives under the influence of the old nature, that is the sinful nature of the unconverted person. Names given to the old nature in Scripture are as follows: "the natural man" (that is "a man without God's Spirit", *NIV*); "the old man" (or "old self", *NIV*); "the outward man" (1 Corinthians 2:14; 2 Corinthians 4:16; Ephesians 4:22).

However, for us who have accepted the Lord Jesus as our Saviour, our walk forward from God's standpoint is in the Spirit. "Spirit" is translated from the Greek word *pneuma*, which is used extensively in God's Word, particularly of the invisible God and His operations. For example: "God is Spirit" (John 4:24). But "Spirit" in this case is the Spirit which is given by God to the believer at conversion—a divine Spirit.

When we walk in the Spirit we conduct our lives under the influence of the new nature which has been created in us by God. It is in direct contrast to the old nature and for this reason is termed as the following: "divine nature"; "the new man" or "new creation"; "the inward man" (or "inner being", *NIV*); (2 Peter 1:4; Ephesians 4:24; 2 Corinthians 5:17; Romans 7:22).

In this publication it is my aim to make a comparison of both these states by considering different aspects of the two natures of the believer from the teaching in Scripture. As we cover facets of doctrine on this subject from different viewpoints, it is very probable that some repetition may occur. Even so, such scrutiny will reveal to us just how contrary the old nature is to the new nature and the reasons why. Following this we can look at some practical applications on how we ought to behave with respect to these two natures, in order that our outlook might be the right one with God.

The Old Nature

versus

The New Nature

The Old Nature
versus
The New Nature

If you are a true believer in God then you will undergo the experience of inner conflict, as did the Apostle Paul—please read Romans 7:13-25. Whilst these verses of Scripture may seem quite involved, let us focus on the struggle that Paul here describes owing to having two natures dwelling within him side by side—that is the old nature and the new nature. He speaks of a warring in his body members against the law of his mind.

This battle that Paul experiences is between the old Saul, who is still very much present, and the new Paul, which was the result of his miraculous conversion that he underwent whilst on the road to Damascus, when he received a vision of the ascended Lord. The explanation for the wrestling that Paul, or any believer, undergoes is because the old nature, which is a sinful nature, and the new nature, which is a divine nature, are

bear the characteristics of God's Son—a divine nature which is righteous and holy. We need to reckon ourselves as having died to sin and being alive in Christ. We are to walk forward in the Spirit and behave as though we are already there in the spiritual realms with God in Christ (Colossians 3:1-3). The presence of the flesh is not an excuse for walking in it. We are called to put to death our members which are on the earth (v 5). In other words we should keep them down or subdue them and by doing this we will not fulfil the lusts or desires of the flesh (or sinful nature).

The Apostle Paul in his conflict cries out, "O wretched man that I am! Who will deliver me from this body of death?", and his new spiritual being provides the answer—"I thank God—through Jesus Christ our Lord!" (Romans 7:24-25). Acceptance of Jesus Christ into our lives as our Saviour is the cause of our conflict, but He is the One who will deliver us from it at the appointed time.

In the meantime we must struggle on with this warfare raging within us, but we can rejoice knowing that this is a means to an end—the battle is as good as won and the victory already accomplished. Therefore, we can join Paul and offer our thanks to God who has given us the victory through Jesus Christ our Lord.

The Old Birth

versus

The New Birth

The Old Birth
versus
The New Birth

That which is born of the flesh is flesh, and that which is born of the Spirit is spirit. (John 3:6)

Jesus said, "A woman, when she is in labour, has sorrow because her hour has come; but as soon as she has given birth to the child, she no longer remembers the anguish, for joy that a human being has been born into the world" (John 16:21). Any mother knows the above words of Jesus to be true. The birth of a baby son or daughter is indeed a joyous occasion.

Our physical birth is the beginning of our life on this natural earth, the home God has provided for us. But from a very early age it becomes very apparent that something is amiss in our behaviour. The Apostle Paul in his experience was moved to say, "For I know that in me (that is, in my flesh) nothing good dwells" (Romans 7:18).

Let us see what some Old Testament characters have to say about our natural birth. *David* – "Behold, I was brought forth in iniquity, and in sin my mother conceived me" (Psalm 51:5). *Bildad* (Job's companion) – "How then can man be righteous before God? Or how can he be pure who is born of woman?" (Job 25:4). *Job* – "Man who is born of woman is of few days and full of trouble" (Job 14:1); also "Who can bring a clean thing out of an unclean?" (v 4). Both Job and Jeremiah cursed the day of their birth (Job 3:3; Jeremiah 20:14). All these were unanimous in the fact that because of our inherent fallen nature, every person born of woman falls short of the glory of God (Romans 3:23).

In the flesh we shall remain as corrupt as the day we were born. As innocent as we may have looked as new-born babes, we were born in corruption, and no amount of effort on our part can ever change this. We can never make holy what is already impaired. In the flesh we can never please God (Romans 8:8). But God was not happy to leave us in this sorry state. Therefore, in and through the birth of a male child, He made provision in order that the sad situation could be changed.

Isaiah prophesied of this birth when he said, "For unto us a child is born, unto us a Son is given" (9:6). This prophecy was fulfilled when at His birth the angel of the Lord announced His arrival to shepherds in the fields when they said, "For there is born to you this day in the City of David a Saviour, who is Christ the Lord" (Luke 2:11). The birth of the Christ-child was very different to all other births since Adam, because Mary, His mother, conceived Him by God's Holy Spirit.

At His birth, He assumed a complete human nature that was in union with the divine— Godhead and manhood inseparably joined in one person—Jesus Christ. The angel had said to Mary, "that Holy One who is to be born will be called the Son of God" (Luke 1:35). Because God was the Father of this child, He did not inherit Adam's fallen nature. It was necessary for Him to come to us in the flesh, because it was in this state that the Holy One of God, who was set apart from sinners, was able and willing to offer

His own holy life on our behalf. This He did when at His death He took upon Himself all our sins and died in our place. Jesus Christ, the Son of God, condemned sin in His own body of flesh and made it possible for us to become righteous in God's sight. But God did not allow His Holy One to see corruption. He raised Him up and He became the *firstborn from the dead* that He might have pre-eminence or first place in a new spiritual creation into which believers can enter by faith.

Jesus said to Nicodemus, "Unless one is born again, he cannot see the kingdom of God" (John 3:3). Entrance into God's new creation, which was inaugurated by Christ's resurrection, means we must first undergo a new birth in the Spirit. We must be "born of the Spirit." In the way that our natural birth in the flesh was the beginning of our physical life on this earth, our new birth in the Spirit is the beginning of a new life with God in Christ in the Spirit. Receiving Christ as our Saviour gives us the right to become children of God, because our new birth is not of blood, nor of the will of the flesh, nor of the will of man, but of God (John 1:12-13). We are born of God and have become a new creation by receiving the seal of God's Holy Spirit.

God has demonstrated His great love for us by saving us from the fate of our old sinful nature in the flesh, which was of corruptible seed, and making us partakers of His own spiritual nature, which is of incorruptible seed, and is therefore righteous and holy (1 Peter 1:23). Because these two natures are opposites they are pulling in different directions—"that which is born of the flesh" and "that which is born of the Spirit" (John 3:6). In Galatians 4:21-31, the births of Abraham's two sons, Ishmael and Isaac, are used symbolically to illustrate the difference between the flesh and the Spirit, and the enmity that exists. As it says, he who was born according to the flesh persecuted him who was born according to the Spirit. And so it is with our natures within. The old constantly badgers the new. However, our new birth has lifted us to the heavenly realms so that we can enter the kingdom of God (John 3:5).

The Origin and Character of the Old Nature

versus

The Origin and Character of the New Nature

The Origin and Character of the Old Nature

versus

The Origin and Character of the New Nature

Having differentiated between the old natural birth in the flesh and the new birth in the Spirit, it seems appropriate to consider the origins of both these natures and also their character. As we do so this will emphasise the contrast between the two and help us to understand why they are not compatible.

1 Corinthians 15:45-49 is a passage that will help us here. These verses introduce two characters, the first man Adam, and the Last Adam (Jesus Christ), and they tell us that we are to bear the image of both.

The first is the natural man who is of the earth—made of dust. From the elements found in the dust of the earth God made man and when He breathed into his nostrils the breath of life, he became a living being (Genesis 2:7). God created Adam, the first man, a real physical human being made of flesh and blood, and we at our natural birth, because we are his offspring, bear the image of the man of dust. As descendants of Adam, not only were we born with a body of flesh and blood like his, but we also bear all the characteristics of his fallen state, which was the consequence of his disobedience to God.

The second is the spiritual man. In these verses He is called the *second Man* or the *last Adam,* who is the Lord from heaven. The Lord Jesus, He is the One who came down from heaven and made it possible for us to become like Him and bear His image and character.

After His death and resurrection He became a life giving Spirit and made it possible for us to receive a rebirth in the Spirit, as we considered in the last section, which is a new creation. These verses in 1 Corinthians 15 are dealing with resurrection and look forward to the day when our new spiritual being receives a spiritual body that is compatible with its nature. It likens our new nature to an incorruptible seed which will one day be clothed upon with a body from heaven. However, in the meantime, the new spiritual nature we received from God is a guarantee of our hope to come, and also a foretaste of our future spiritual heavenly life with God in Christ.

As a descendant of Adam, the natural man is only capable of walking according to the ways of the world, fulfilling the desires of the flesh. Because of this he is described as being by nature a child of wrath (Ephesians 2:1-3). No matter how hard we try to improve, refine or cultivate the old nature by education, or works of righteousness etc., we can never reach the high moral standard of God. Neither can we measure ourselves by comparing our behaviour with others who seem to have done much worse than we have. The question is, "how do we measure up in God's sight?"

When the prophet Isaiah saw the Lord in all His glory, he exclaimed, "Woe is me, for I am

undone! Because I am a man of unclean lips …..
for my eyes have seen the King, the Lord of
Hosts" (Isaiah 6:5). We all, in our sinful nature,
fall short of God's glory. When we contrast
ourselves with God's holiness the conclusion is,
as the Apostle Paul came to realise, that in the
flesh nothing good dwells (Romans 7:18).

In contrast, the origin and character of the new
spiritual man that we derived from the heavenly
man, is a nature that is created in the image of
Christ (Colossians 3:10). Ephesians 4:24 tells us
that the *new man* was created to be like God, in
righteousness and true holiness. Even as our old
nature is hopelessly bad, our new nature is pure,
good, perfect and holy and incapable of sin (1
John 3:9), because it comes from the One who is
sinless and holy.

The natural man craves after the things of the
earth from where he came, but in contrast our
new spiritual man desires heavenly things,
because he came from the Lord in heaven, and
that is where he is heading to be forever with

Him. For our citizenship is in heaven from where we eagerly await our Saviour (Philippians 3:20).

The origins of both these natures help us to understand why they are incongruous. They are not happy to coexist in unison because they are from completely different sources and are also heading in different directions.

Sons of Man

versus

Sons of God

Sons of Man
versus
Sons of God

Scriptural teaching is that every man born of woman claims his ancestry from Adam, the first man—the man of dust. As descendants of Adam, we are by nature designated sons of Adam (Deuteronomy 32:8) or sons of man (Ecclesiastes 1:13; Ephesians 3:5). Even though God created man a little lower than the angels, He still gave to him glory, honour and power over all His other earthly creatures. He made him in His own image and according to His own likeness and gave to him dominion over the works of His hands (Psalm 8:4-8). Even so, Adam in such a privileged position was not content to put his trust in God and His word when the time of testing came, but gave his allegiance to another.

Through the fall of Adam, this dominion was forfeited until the One whose right it is comes to rule over the earth. By his actions Adam cast not only himself, but also all his future offspring, outside the family of God. By his disobedience he caused all his seed to be named "sons of disobedience" subject to the judgement of God (Ephesians 2:1-3).

Therefore, by descent and nature of our birth, in God's estimation we are described as being "dead in trespasses and sins" (Ephesians 2:1). However, verse 4 reveals a reversal of the situation when it states: "But God, who is rich in mercy, because of His great love with which He loved us, even when we were dead in trespasses, made us alive together with Christ." Even though such a disastrous beginning had set man off on the wrong footing, as it were, God still loved mankind whom He had created. Through His rich mercy and great love, God not only brought us from the state of being dead to being alive, but also enabled the fallen sons of Adam to become children or even sons of God.

The Psalmist said, "What is man that You are mindful of him, and the son of man that You visit him" (Psalm 8:4). But the Lord, the great Creator, was very mindful of man. He did visit this earthly planet, the home of sinful man. This He did in His Son, Jesus Christ, who not only claimed for Himself the title Son of God, but also became identified with man by becoming the Son of Man (Matthew 8:20), but with a difference— without sin.

As the Son of Man, or the "last Adam", Jesus, unlike Adam, overcame all temptation. He suffered and became obedient even unto death, when He gave Himself at Calvary for man's sin. But the Father did not allow His "Holy One" to see corruption in the burial tomb but raised Him from the dead. When Acts 13:33-34 speaks of Jesus' resurrection, it quotes from Psalm 2:7 when the Father said: "You are My Son, today I have begotten You." Jesus Christ, God's only begotten, became the first begotten from the dead (Revelation 1:5 *KJV*). Romans 1:4 says that He was declared to be the Son of God with power, in and through the Spirit of holiness, by the resurrection from the dead.

Because Christ became the Creator and initiator of a new spiritual creation at His resurrection, believers are not only born again, but in this receive a rebirth as children or sons of God. By His work of atonement, Christ has reconciled sinful man back into the family of God—that is if we believe in Him and His work. John 1:12-13 tells us that those believers who received Him, to them He gave the right to become children of God.

The Apostle John said, "Behold what manner of love the Father has bestowed on us, that we should be called children of God!" (1 John 3:1). John in his writings uses the Greek word *teknon* (child) for the believer, whereas the Apostle Paul also uses *huios* (a son), when he introduces his teaching on adoption. Whilst John's ministry brings the believer into the family of faith, Paul in his teaching, takes a further step forward by giving the believer the position of son-ship with special privileges with a guaranteed inheritance in view.

At conversion, a transferral of family and status takes place for the believer. We are transferred from the headship of Adam, the sinful man, to the headship of Christ, the Holy One. This is possible because as Romans 8:15 explains, when we believed we received the spirit of adoption by whom we can cry out "Abba Father", which is the cry of a true son. Galatians 4:6 says, "Because you are sons, God has sent the Spirit of His Son into your hearts, crying out 'Abba, Father!'"

Receiving the Holy Spirit as a seal or pledge, is what enables us to become true sons of God and bears witness with our own spirit that we are indeed children of God (Romans 8:16). It is a Son-ship Spirit or divine Spirit (Greek - *Pneuma-Christou*, v 9) that we receive from God, which makes us accepted in the Beloved and enables us to enjoy fellowship with God through His own Beloved Son.

The special relationship that we can now enjoy with the Father, through His Son, includes His care and protection and even His chastening when we do wrong, but He never casts us off. It brings with it the privileges and also the responsibilities that true sons/daughters receive from the Father and also, as mentioned earlier, an inheritance to come. Ephesians 1:11 says, "In whom also we have obtained an inheritance, being predestined according to the purpose of Him who works all things according to the counsel of His will." Our inheritance to come is said to be at God's own right hand in the heavenly places, far above all (Ephesians 1:20-23; 2:6).

The Sinful Nature

versus

The Divine Nature

The Sinful Nature
versus
The Divine Nature

Even though we are made to be God's children or sons on the basis of faith in and through Christ, our problems are not yet over. In this section we are going to consider more closely what the Scriptures say about the opposing natures of our old being and our new spiritual being. In the Oxford Dictionary, one definition of the word *nature* is the following: "inherent impulses determining character or actions", which is a good example for our purpose.

So far, when we have spoken of the old nature, we have associated it with sin and also Adam's disobedience—that it was through one man that sin entered. It is in Genesis 3 that we read the story of Adam and Eve, the first man and woman, and of their fall. As well as receiving God-given dominion over all God's earthly creatures, also given into Adam's care was the woman whom God had created to be a helper suitable for him. With respect to their disobedience, whilst 1 Timothy 2:13-14 tells us that it was the woman who was deceived, even so it was Adam who failed to protect the woman whom God had put into his care. Adam disobeyed open-eyed knowing the consequence of his actions. But also behind their disobedience was the one who had deceived Eve, the serpent, identified in Revelation 12:7-9 as the devil himself. He was the one who had sinned from the beginning (1 John 3:8).

As God had declared to Adam and Eve, death was a consequence of sin (Genesis 2:17), and was genetically passed down to all mankind (Romans 5:12). Because of this the Apostle John was moved to say that the whole world lies under the power of the wicked one (1 John 5:19). Even God's nation Israel, whom He had redeemed and set apart to be His own, were described as being "a people laden with iniquity", whose sins were likened to scarlet (Isaiah 1:4,18).

Sin separates us from the Most Holy God, and also condemns us in His presence. If we walk in the sinful nature that we inherited from our ancestors, we are unable to please God (Romans 8:8) because it is dominated by works that are contrary to the Spirit. These works are classified in Galatians 5:19-21 as being: adultery, fornication, uncleanness … hatred, contentions, jealousies, outbursts of wrath, selfish ambition etc. Therefore, Ephesians 4:22-24 instructs us to put off the old man and its deeds, and in its place put on the new man, which was created to be like God in righteousness and true holiness. (See also Colossians 3:1-14.)

The nature of the new man, that we are instructed to put on and which was given us when we believed, is not generated from Adam, but generated from Christ, by nature of our new birth. When Colossians 3:10 instructs us to put on the new man, it tells us that he is renewed in the knowledge and in the image of his creator, who is Christ. Therefore, the nature of our new creation is not only derived from Christ, but is also in His image. Christ, in God's Word, is characterised as follows: The Holy One and the Just (Luke 1:35; Acts 3:14); without sin, undefiled and separate from sinners (Hebrews 4:15; 7:26); He knew no sin (2 Corinthians 5:21); without spot and blemish (Hebrews 9:14; 1 Peter 1:19); Who committed no sin (1 Peter 2:22); righteous (1 John 2:29); In Him is no sin (1 John 3:5).

The nature that comes from Christ is a divine nature. 2 Peter 1:4 tells us that when God called us in faith we became partakers of the divine nature. The divine nature cannot produce sin as a fruit because it comes from God who is holy and righteous. It can only produce love as a fruit and its derivatives (see Galatians 5:22-23). This is what John teaches us in his letters. He says, "And you know that He (Christ) was manifested to take away our sins, and in Him there is no sin. Whoever abides in Him does not sin …" (1 John 3:5-6).

He continues, "whoever has been born of God does not sin, for His (Christ's) seed remains in him; and he cannot sin, because he has been born of God" (v 9). When we believed in Christ as our Saviour, we died to sin and are therefore no longer under its reign or its condemnation. Because we are now in Christ, our walk is now in the Spirit (Romans 8:1)—that is according to God's reckoning.

Therefore, in our new nature it is impossible for us to sin—it is sinless like Christ Himself. When we lapse into sin, we can only do this in the old nature which keeps raising its head and shouting to us, "I'm still here!" But whilst it can have short lapses of triumph, these need be only temporary because God has already given us the victory in and through Christ Jesus. He is the One who now rules our life by the spirit of His love, and love conquers all! God receives us and accepts us only in our new spiritual attire, which is the righteousness and holiness with which we are now clothed, in and through Christ.

Therefore, when we contrast the nature of our old being with the nature of our new creation, we can see that they are extreme opposites. No matter how good our intentions are, deeds done in and through the old nature cannot produce fruit that merits entry into God's kingdom. The old nature can only produce fruits of the flesh, of fallen man. However, the new nature is incapable of sin because it is pure and holy, like Christ, and produces love as its fruit, in which we should live and walk (Galatians 5:22-25).

The Present State of
the Old Nature

versus

The Present State of
the New Nature

The Present State of the Old Nature

versus

The Present State of the New Nature

I am going to use a verse of Scripture as the premise for this section, which is 2 Corinthians 4:16. It begins by saying, "Therefore we do not lose heart. Even though our outward man is perishing ..." As mentioned in the introduction, the term "outward man" is another expression for the old nature—it is perishing! The old nature inhabits a body that is also affected by Adam's sin.

Both the old nature, and the body of flesh and blood it inhabits, are perishing and will die. If we are truthful and face up to reality, we could say from the moment of our birth we are on a course that leads to death. Once we have grown up to maturity, we are then led on a path that is a downward spiral as year by year our physical strength weakens, our body does not operate the way it used to, our thinking pattern slows down, our bones begin to creak, and the dreaded wrinkles appear.

Whilst a lot can be done to slow down this process by good living, eating, sleeping habits and the right kind of exercise, sooner or later it overtakes us. Dwelling on this decline is not recommended for daily living, but rather to enjoy the good things in life whilst we have them, is a better policy. Even so, it is the reality of the situation. We cannot forget the many who have the misfortune of inheriting genetic illnesses, as well as an hereditary sinful nature from our ancestors, which means they live a life that is a constant struggle both physically and spiritually. The outward man is indeed perishing!

The outward man is definitely burdensome. The Apostle Paul was moved to say, "For we who are in this tent (earthly body) groan, being burdened …" (2 Corinthians 5:4). In fact in Romans 8:22, he includes all creation in this groaning. "For we know that the whole creation groans and labours with birth pangs together until now." In the next verse he also brings the believer into this groaning when he says, "And not only they, but we also who have the firstfruits of the Spirit, even we ourselves groan within ourselves, eagerly waiting for the adoption, the redemption of our body."

Whilst we continue on in this earthly tent (body), we desire a body that is not weighed down by physical infirmities and spiritual weaknesses, which are the trappings of the outward man (old nature). In the days of Jesus, the people flocked to Him to be healed of their sicknesses. Such healings took place for just a few years, because they pointed forward to the days when God's kingdom will indeed rule the earth and bring permanent cures to man's ills.

What then do the Scriptures say about the future of the natural man? God said to Adam following his rebellion, "For dust you are, and to dust you shall return" (Genesis 3:19). Elihu (Job's comforter) reasoned that, "If He (God) should gather to Himself His Spirit and His breath, all flesh would perish together, and man would return to dust" Job 34:14-15). Solomon's recommendation was to remember your Creator in the days of your youth, before the difficult days come. Solomon then goes on to describe in allegorical terms the breakdown process that eventually leads to the day when the dust would return to the earth and the spirit would return to God who gave it (Ecclesiastes 12:1-7).

The days of the man of flesh and blood in Scripture are likened to the following:-

All flesh is as grass ….. The grass withers, and its flower falls away. (1 Peter 1:24)

Our days on earth are as a shadow, and without hope.
(1 Chronicles 29:15)

For what is your life? It is even a vapour that appears for a little time and then vanishes away. (James 4:14)

The Psalmist said, "The days of our lives are seventy years; And if by reason of strength they are eighty years … for it is soon cut off, and we fly away" (Psalm 90:10). The above sections of Scripture give no indication of hope, because they are speaking only of the future of the physical man—that is the man without God's Spirit and without Christ (as indeed the Gentiles, as well as the Jews, were before conversion - Romans 8:9; Ephesians 2:12).

Let us now return to the Scripture that we considered at the beginning of this section (2 Corinthians 4:16). "Even though our outward man is perishing, yet the *inward man* is being renewed day by day". The *inward man* is another expression for the new nature or *new man* that we received at conversion which has a future hope.

Our old man or nature is on a downward spiral and is perishing. In contrast, our new nature is being constantly nourished and renewed by God's Holy Spirit with strength and power from the One who supplies all our spiritual needs. In Ephesians and Colossians the church of believers is spoken of as the Body of Christ with Christ as the Head. The whole church receives nourishment and is knit together by the Head who is Christ (Ephesians 4:15,16).

And every believer who is a member of this church receives constant renewal from God's Holy Spirit, who is in Himself a power source of life in and through Christ, who dwells in our heart through faith. That is why even though our outward man may be weak and sickly, our inward man or being can feel strong and healthy.

We have a good example of this in the Apostle Paul who was experiencing a problem that he described as being 'a thorn in the flesh'. We are not told what this problem actually was, but it was obviously causing Paul some distress resulting in a conflict between the flesh and the Spirit, the flesh on this occasion eclipsing Paul's joy—hence his pleading to God for its removal. It was Christ's answer to Paul's pleading that changed Paul's outlook when He said, "My grace is sufficient for you, for My strength is made perfect in weakness" (2 Corinthians 12:9).

We can note the difference in Paul's way of thinking after Christ had strengthened him by His grace in the inner man, by Paul's answer: "Therefore, I take pleasure in infirmities, in reproaches, in needs, in persecutions, in distresses for Christ's sake. For when I am weak, then I am strong" (v 10).

A person's spiritual state or strength is not based on his/her ability to cope with mental and physical hardships. But rather it depends on our submission to Christ and allowing Him to carry us through, as did Paul.

It is when we are experiencing life's problems that weigh us down and weaken us that Christ's strength can be made perfect in our weakness, if we only turn to Him. When we do this the inner man becomes the dominant force in our lives and the outer man is kept subdued and in its proper place.

The Apostle Paul found in the course of his ministry that no matter what situation he found himself to be in, whether favourable or unfavourable, the latter often the case, that he could do all things through Christ who strengthened him (Philippians 4:13; 2 Timothy 4:17). Christ did this, as He also does for us, through the renewing day by day with His grace and strength through His Holy Spirit in us.

The Holy Spirit has life in Himself because it is the Spirit of Christ and God who is the source of all life who dwells in our heart. Therefore, even though the outward man is perishing, we do not lose heart, because we know that the affliction we experience is temporary, but God's working in us through the inner man brings everlasting glory.

Slavery of the Old Nature

Versus

Freedom of the New Nature

Slavery of the Old Nature *versus* Freedom of the New Nature

The sinfulness of the old nature inherited from Adam is the reason why it is perishing. It is in bondage to sin and corruption. It makes us slaves of sin, which results in death, and reigns over and controls our lives. It is incapable of reaching the high moral standards of God. Therefore, says Romans 3:23, "For all have sinned and fall short of the glory of God."

Therefore, in the old nature, sin is what we are. Paul in his letters speaks not only of 'sin' which is the state of the old nature, but also of 'sins', which are the fruits of that nature—the inborn tendency to commit deeds contrary to the will of God. Jesus said to the Jews, "whoever commits sin is a slave of sin" (John 8:34), and the Apostle Paul spoke about the believer's former state as being 'slaves of sin' (Romans 6:17). Paul spoke about his own position when he allowed his fleshly nature to raise its head. He said, "But I see another law in my members, warring against the law of my mind, and bringing me into captivity to the law of sin which is in my members" (Romans 7:23). Because of this Paul reasoned that in the flesh he served the law of sin (v 25).

The Scriptures speak of the reason and also several ways in which the old nature and its works hold its victim in bondage or slavery:

The Devil: First, the devil is the one who caused the state of the old nature by his opposition to God and his deception of Eve. He is the true master of the old nature and whilst we serve sin we also serve the devil and do his will rather than God's (2 Timothy 2:26).

The World: Galatians 4:3 speaks of the children of this age as being in bondage under the elements of this world. The Apostle John said that the whole world is lying under the sway of the wicked one (1 John 5:19). That is why he encouraged believers not to love the world or the things in it. He said, "For all that is in the world—the lust of the flesh, the lust of the eyes, and the pride of life—is not of the Father, but is of the world" (1 John 2:15-16); and these are the things that hold us in bondage.

False Teachers:

What does come from the world, in the form of religion, are false teachers who lure their converts into groups or theologies which hold them captive by false teachings, especially concerning the identity of the Saviour. Both the Apostle Peter and the Apostle Paul warned of such.

Peter said that by promising liberty they lead those who are overcome by them into bondage, becoming slaves of corruption as they themselves already were (2 Peter 2:19).

Paul likewise warned the church to be on the watch for such false apostles who transformed themselves into the apostles of Christ and he added, "no wonder! For Satan himself transforms himself into an angel of light" (2 Corinthians 11:1-15—see also Galatians 2:1-4).

The Law:

Paul, in his letters to the Romans and Galatians, had need to reprimand the Jewish Christians with respect to Law and grace. Having been redeemed he said that they desired again to be in bondage (Galatians 4:9). He likened the Old Law Covenant to Hagar saying it gives birth to bondage (v 24). Whilst the Law did reveal grace, it was only typical of true grace, along with its types and shadows (John 1:16). It was only a shadow of good things to come (Hebrews 10:1). There was nothing wrong with the Law itself. Even Paul said it was holy, just and good (Romans 7:12).

It was decreed by God and served a purpose until the appointed time, at the end of the Acts, when it was abolished (Ephesians 2:14-16; Colossians 2:14-17). The problem was with those who were under it. It was impossible for fallen man to keep because it required perfect obedience. Galatians

3:10 says, "Cursed is everyone who does not continue in *all* things which are written in the book of the law, to do them."

As Paul reasoned this out, he reminded them that the Law was added because of transgressions until the seed of promise should come (Galatians 3:19). And that by the Law was the knowledge of sin (Romans 3:20). In other words the Law made those under it more aware of their sin and also of their need for a Saviour to deliver them from it. Therefore, from this viewpoint, those under the Law were brought under curse and in bondage with no hope of ever being able to do it perfectly. By the works of the Law no man could be justified before God (Galatians 2:16).

Sin and Death:

Paul continued to reason on the subject of the Law in this way, "And the commandment, which was to bring life, I found to bring death" (Romans 7:10). Through the working of the Law the knowledge of sin was brought to the fore. He continued, "For we know that the Law is spiritual, but I am carnal, sold under sin" (Romans 7:14); and being slaves of sin leads to death (Romans 6:16,23). Fear of death brings with it a lifetime of bondage says Hebrews 2:15, and is, therefore, something that we need deliverance from.

Whilst the old nature is held in bondage to sin and corruption resulting in death, the new spiritual nature brings freedom. The seal of God's Holy Spirit that we received when we believed is not a spirit of bondage says Romans 8:15. We have been called to liberty and we are instructed to stand fast in it. As the old nature derived from Adam brought us into bondage, the new nature derived from Christ sets us free. Therefore, says John 8:36, "If the Son makes you free, you shall be free indeed."

Freedom from the Devil:

The freedom that Christ gives sets us free from the hold of our old master, the devil. In the new nature we are set free to do God's will and serve Him (1 Peter 2:15-16; Romans 6:22). Colossians

3:24, on the subject of the character of the *new man* says, "we serve the Lord Christ". He is the Master of our new nature. The old man has no choice but is automatically held captive and bound by Satan, but by putting our faith in Christ as our Saviour we choose to serve our new Master, Christ. Therefore we serve Him in freedom and not as slaves but even as sons (Galatians 4:7).

Freedom from the World:

When we received the promised Holy Spirit, we did not receive the spirit of the world (1 Corinthians 2:12), but the Spirit who is from God. At that time we were delivered from the powers of darkness, which control the world we are living in today, and we were translated into the Kingdom of the Son of God's love (Colossians 1:13). Therefore, from a spiritual viewpoint, we are not part of the world.

Whilst at the present time we are not taken physically out of the world, we have the assurance that whilst we walk forward in the *new man,* we will be kept from the evil one; (see Christ's prayer for His disciples in John 17:9-26). The Apostle James said, "Friendship with the world is enmity with God" (James 4:4). Therefore we must keep ourselves unspotted from the world (James 1:27).

Freedom from False Teachers:

The aim of the false apostles who had infiltrated the Christian congregation was to bring the Christian Jews again into bondage (Galatians 2:4). Paul, when writing to the Corinthians, tells them how to identify such false teachers by looking out for three specific areas of teaching. He warns them to be on the watch for anyone who comes to them and preaches *another Jesus* whom we have not preached, or if they bring a *different spirit,* which you have not received.

And lastly, if they preach a *different gospel,* which you have not accepted (2 Corinthians 11:4). And so today we can link these areas of false teaching to many cults and religious groups, who deny the Deity of Jesus Christ by preaching *another Jesus,* who preach an impersonal 'holy spirit', and also a gospel that propagates works for salvation. Receiving the Spirit of truth, which is the new nature, when our eyes were opened to the saving knowledge of our Saviour and His true gospel, cuts the chains of such false teachers and sets us free from teachings that lead us into bondage, which are the fruits of such false teachers. The acid test of all teaching claimed to be of the Holy Spirit is 'does it glorify Christ'? (John 16:14).

Freedom from the Curse of the Law:

Paul said to the Galatian Christians, "the law was our tutor to bring us to Christ, that we might be justified by faith" (Galatians 3:24). And that by this, "Christ has redeemed us from the curse of the law" (Galatians 3:13). Receiving the promised Holy Spirit (v 14) released them from being under the yoke of bondage, which was the curse of the Law, and brought them under grace. Whilst the Christian Jews of the Acts period still needed to keep the Law, as we find Paul and his disciples often times doing, it wasn't their means of salvation. Jesus Christ was. Whilst today we are not under the Law, we are still in danger of becoming trapped by regulations and traditions of men (Colossians 2:20-23) and it is the old nature that loves such things. By walking forward in the *new creation* we shall not be held by such rules and regulations and will enjoy the peace and blessing of God.

Freedom from the law of sin and death:

Paul, when speaking of the believer's walk in the Spirit said the following, "For the law of the Spirit of life in Christ Jesus has made me free from the law of sin and death" (Romans 8:2). "The wages of sin is death" (Romans 6:23) but God sent His own Son on account of sin, to pay for sin, and satisfy His own righteous judgement, and in this bring us from death to life. Christ paid the price for our deliverance. "Christ died for our sins ….. He was buried and ….. He rose again the third day" (1 Corinthians 15:3-4).

From a spiritual viewpoint, Paul in Romans 6:1-4, speaks of the believer's identification with Christ in His death, burial, and resurrection, bringing us from the state of being dead in sin to being alive in God through Jesus Christ and with it freedom from sin and its enslavement (v 7). Even though, from a physical viewpoint, we must still face death to actually free us from the old nature or man, nevertheless we will not die in our sins, but be saved out of death through the resurrection on the appointed day. For the believer the sting has been taken out of death (1 Corinthians 15:55).

With these things in view we are told to stand fast in the liberty by which Christ has made us free. We should use this liberty to serve not only God, but also one another in and through love (Galatians 5:1,13).

The Heart and Mind of the Old Nature

Versus

The Heart and Mind of the New Nature

The Heart and Mind of the Old Nature
versus
The Heart and Mind of the New Nature

Even though as believers we now walk forward in freedom, we still undergo inner conflict as mentioned at the introduction of this booklet. The reason for this is because when God made us a new creation at conversion, this included a new heart and mind which are in conflict with the heart and mind of our old nature.

When we consider the Scriptures that speak about the heart of man, we soon begin to see that they are not talking about an organ that pumps blood around the body but rather about the seat of motivation. In the Scriptures the heart and mind are sometimes spoken of independently, but other times linked together as in Psalm 7:9 and Psalm 26:2. In the latter King David is inviting the Lord to examine him and test his heart and mind. This is because out of the heart can come both good and bad. But David was described as being a man after God's own heart (1 Samuel 13:14; Acts 13:22).

He was also described (along with others) as having a heart that was perfect (or loyal) toward God. This did not mean that he always did everything right because we know that this was not so, but he never gave his worship or allegiance to another. He was always faithful in his worship. The greatest commandment given to God's people was, to "love the Lord your God with all your heart, with all your soul and with all your mind" (Matthew 22:37). And we can only do this if our heart is right with God.

The Heart and Mind of the Old Nature (Natural Man)

The Scriptures that speak about the condition of the heart of the natural unconverted man are very forthright. For example in Jeremiah 17:9 it says, "The heart is deceitful above all things, and desperately wicked." Other Scriptures tell us that it is wayward, is full of iniquity, is hard, is proud, is malicious, is covetous, is foolish and so we could continue. The Lord Jesus Himself said, "For out of the heart proceed evil thoughts, murders, adulteries, fornications, thefts, false witness, blasphemies" (Matthew 15:19). What about the mind?

The thoughts of the carnal mind are opposite to God's thoughts—"Because the carnal mind is enmity against God; for it is not subject to the law of God, nor indeed can be" (Romans 8:7). The carnal mind is not subject to the law of God but to the law of flesh, fulfilling the desires of the flesh, and as a consequence brings us under judgement. In other words the mind of the adamic man is incapable of coming near to or pleasing God. He said, "My thoughts are not your thoughts, nor are your ways My ways" (Isaiah 55:8).

God is the assessor, evaluator, of all hearts. In 1 Chronicles 28:9 it says, "for the Lord searches all hearts and understands all the intent of the thoughts. If you seek Him, He will be found by you." It is very unnerving to know that the Lord knows the secrets of our hearts (Psalm 44:21) and the thoughts of man (Psalm 94:11). When a dispute arose among Jesus' disciples, Luke 9:47 tells us that Jesus perceived the thoughts of their hearts. Even though the heart and mind of the unregenerate man is unable to come anywhere near the righteous thoughts of the most holy God, even so God is searching hearts for those who are looking for Him. The Lord is particularly near those who have a broken heart and it is His desire to save such as those who have a contrite spirit (Psalm 34:18). What happens then when He finds someone whose heart is penitent—someone who truly feels sorry about the wrong thoughts aroused from the heart? Because the Lord knows the thoughts and intents of man, He knows when such sorrow is genuine. Even so we still need the touch of God to open our hearts to find Him (see 1 Samuel 10:26; Acts 16:14). This is when conversion takes place and we receive God's Spirit that brings about our new creation. This is also when God creates in us a new heart and mind which are righteous and holy.

God knows that the heart of the natural man cannot be changed. Speaking of the Nation of Israel who will repent at the end of this era when they see the Lord whom they pierced come in all His glory to save them (read Zechariah 12:10-14), what does God say to them? He says, "I will give you a new heart and put a new spirit within you; I will take the heart of stone out of your flesh and give you a heart of flesh" (Ezekiel 36:26; 11:19). In the way that the glory of the Lord at His coming will awaken Israel to repentance, it is the same light that has shone in our hearts to enlighten us to the knowledge of His glory in the face of Jesus Christ (2 Corinthians 4:6).

The Heart and Mind of the New Creation

In contrast to the condition of the heart of the old man, the heart of the *new man* in the Scriptures is described as being obedient (Ephesians 6:5-6; Romans 6:17-18), believes or has faith (Acts 15:9), is joyful, is pure, is upright, is clean, is holy, is compassionate, is sincere or devout and so we could continue. The thought processing of the *new man* is able to produce actions that are good and holy in God's eyes because it is motivated by love. The new heart we received from God is a heart in which Christ can dwell by faith by His Spirit in us through the inner man (Ephesians 3:16-17), and as a result of this we now can have the mind of Christ (1 Corinthians 2:16). "Let this mind be in you which was also in Christ Jesus", says Philippians 2:5.

Because the heart of our new creation is motivated by the sacrificial love of Christ, this means we can adopt the attitude of Christ such as a willing mind (2 Corinthians 8:12), lowliness or humbleness of mind (Philippians 2:3; Colossians 3:12). We can be of one mind (Philippians 1:27) or of the same mind with our fellow believers (Romans 12:16) as Christ was one with the Father and His disciples (John 17:20-21). Like Christ we can have a mind that truly delights in the law of God (Romans 7:22), and gives us peace and joy to serve Him wholeheartedly in heart and mind.

Here we have a choice that the unconverted person doesn't have. As believers, the workings of the new heart and mind of our new creation should dominate our behaviour and thinking. But because of the presence of the old heart and mind through the old nature, which is still with us, it is possible for us to lapse and fall under its influence. How can we prevent this from happening?

Just as our physical heart needs care and attention if it is to work properly, so does our spiritual heart. Are we carrying about unnecessary weight of burdens and cares instead of giving them to the Lord and trusting Him? As with the pulse, are we keeping to a steady rhythm or pattern of worship and fellowship? Are we feeding it the correct diet of spiritual food provided for in God's Word? Is our heart throbbing with the right thoughts, affections and choices? Let us not be caught out with an unprepared heart (2 Chronicles 12:14), but rather make it a suitable dwelling place for the Lord Himself to feel at home in.

Consequences and End of the Old Nature

versus

Consequences and End of the New Nature

Consequences and End of the Old Nature
versus
Consequences and End of the New Nature

Attired in the old nature our only standing before God is in condemnation with our heads bowed low in shame because of its sinful state. All of mankind, Jew and Gentile alike, is under sin (Romans 3:9). Even God's chosen nation to whom He gave the Law were included in this condemnation, because by the Law was the knowledge of sin, as considered earlier. Therefore, left in this plight all the world stands guilty before God (Romans 3:19-20).

Where then, we might ask, is the old nature leading us? What is its end? "The wages of sin is death" says Romans 6:23. Because of the sinfulness of the old nature, the sentence on the adamic man is death with no hope. If we live only according to the flesh, we will die, says

Romans 8:13. No wonder the Apostle Paul cried out, "O wretched man that I am! Who will deliver me from this body of death?" (Romans 7:24).

Paul then comforts himself with the answer when he says, "I thank God—through Jesus Christ our Lord!" (v 25). Sin reigned through the disobedience of one man resulting in condemnation, but through one Man's righteous act, the gift of righteousness will reign in life through the Man, Jesus Christ (Romans 5:17-19). Christ Jesus stood before God in our shame and when He died He bore our sins in His own body on the tree of Calvary (1 Peter 2:24). The Lord laid on Him the iniquity of us all (Isaiah 53:6).

By the grace of God, the gift of deliverance came through Jesus Christ resulting in righteousness for the recipients. With this in view, Romans 8 opens: "There is therefore now no condemnation to those who are in Christ Jesus." When God receives us, He accepts us in and through His own beloved Son, even in His righteousness and holiness. Saved by grace through faith, we do not need to wait until the day of glory to be sure of redemption because the Spirit of God who raised Jesus from the dead now dwells in us (Romans 8:11). The seal that we received when we believed is our pledge or guarantee of the inheritance to come (Ephesians 1:13-14).

Therefore the consequences and goal of the new nature is peace and life that is eternal, to be ever with our Saviour. Contrary to how death reigned in and through the old nature because of sin, life reigns in and through the new nature because of the work of Christ. This work which includes His death, resurrection, ascension and also His present intercession as He sits at God's right hand, results in a perfect standing before God for us. With this in view the Apostle Paul asks the questions, "who shall bring a charge against God's elect? ... Who is he who condemns? ... Who shall separate us from the love of Christ?" (Romans 8:33-35).

The answer to these questions is that no one or nothing in heaven or on the earth can undo the work Christ has done on our behalf, which justifies us and brings us to peace with God. By Him we have access by faith into God's amazing grace and favour enabling us to stand before Him and rejoice in the glory of God (Romans 5:1-2).

Our way forward therefore is to live by the Spirit and walk in the Spirit (Romans 8:1). At this point it would be good to contrast our former walk in the old sinful person with our present walk in the new spiritual converted person, to see the difference this makes to God's estimation of us:-

A walk in the flesh	versus	A walk in the Spirit
A life of sin that profits nothing	versus	A holy life free from sin
Enemies of God	versus	Reconciled to God
Unable to please God	versus	Pleasing to God
No access to God	versus	No separation from God
Guilty and condemned before God	versus	No condemnation before God
Fulfils the desire of the flesh	versus	Fulfils the law of God
Children of God's wrath	versus	God's sons

Its end is death	*versus*	Its end is life eternal
No hope	*versus*	Hope with the guarantee of eternal life

At the present time we are still bound to our old nature even though we are living and walking forward in the new spiritual nature. Therefore to rid ourselves of it we need to die (or be changed). But because of the work of Christ, when this time comes, we will not die in our sins but in hope, and on that wonderful resurrection day, when He appears, we also will appear with Him in the glory.

To Walk
in the Spirit

To Walk in the Spirit

Having contrasted features of the old nature and the new nature, looking at them from differing viewpoints, we now bring them together and make the following observations with respect to our walk in Christ in the Spirit.

In the last section we made a distinction between a walk in the flesh and a walk in the spirit. In Romans 8:1 (*KJV*, *NKJV*) it states that those who are in Christ Jesus do *not* walk according to the flesh but according to the Spirit. Even though our old sinful nature is still very much with us, our way forward as Christian believers is to walk in the Spirit. This chapter of Romans is very emphatic of the fact that if the Spirit of God dwells in a person, then they are not in the flesh but in the Spirit.

With this in mind, how then do we view the old nature? Romans 6:6 says that when Christ died for our sins, our *old man* (nature) was crucified with Him in order that the body of sin might be done away with, so that we are no longer slaves of sin. Earlier verses explain that we died to sin by being baptised into Christ's death and that we were also raised up with Him to walk in the newness of life. Therefore, from this viewpoint, our former life, dominated by the old nature, ceased and we began a new walk in a different sphere, a spiritual one, dominated by the new nature. Consequently, we must view our old nature as being dead. Our standing before God is now as one justified and righteous. Although the old sinful nature is still present, in God's estimation it is dead. He accepts and sees us in and through Christ. We are a new spiritual person, renewed in knowledge in the image of Christ (Colossians 3:10), and in resurrection we shall be clothed with Christ's righteousness. No matter how unworthy we might feel about ourselves, we must accept God's evaluation of us as though it was already accomplished. God is true to His word. With this in mind, we can walk confidently forward in the Spirit.

Galatians 5:25 says, "If we live in the Spirit, let us also walk in the Spirit." Let us look more closely at what is being said here. First, "If we live in the Spirit": this is what God has done for us in and through Christ Jesus. By His work of redemption He has transferred us into a spiritual sphere in which we now live and walk. Second, "… let us also walk in the Spirit": this, and other Scriptures that we will consider, indicate that it is possible for us, even as Christians, *not* to walk in the Spirit. There could be occasions when we slip back into the ways of the old nature. See also the following:-

Romans 6:4: … just as Christ was raised from the dead by the glory of the Father, even so we also *should* walk in the newness of life.

Romans 13:13-14: Let us walk properly … put on the Lord Jesus Christ, and make no provision for the flesh, to fulfil its lusts.

Galatians 5:16: I say then: Walk in the Spirit, and you shall not fulfil the lust of the flesh.

Ephesians 4:1: I, therefore, the prisoner of the Lord, beseech you to have a walk worthy of the calling with which you were called.

Colossians 2:6: As you have therefore received Christ Jesus the Lord, so walk in Him.

2 Corinthians 5:7-9: For we walk by faith, not by sight … Therefore we make it our aim, whether present or absent, to be well pleasing to Him.

Whilst it is Christ who has made us fit to stand before God, even holy in His sight, the above Scriptures show that there is also a practical side to our walk. To 'walk' indicates activity, so how then do we walk forward in the Spirit in order that we do not fulfil the desires of the old sinful nature which is still with us? The answer to this question is woven in two sets of instructions - 'to put off' and 'to put on'. First, we are to put off our old or former self along with its sinful desires and its acts. Second, and in its place, we are to put on the new man, which is created to be like God in righteousness and true holiness (Ephesians 4:22-24). Consider also the following: "*Put on* love" (Colossians 3:14). "*Put on* the whole armour of God" (Ephesians 6:11). "*Put on* the Lord Jesus Christ" (Romans 13:14).

These are all ways of putting on the new nature created in the image of Christ and a protection from the outside forces of sin and darkness.

Ephesians Chapters 4, 5 and 6 contain practical instructions that will help us to walk worthy of the calling to which we have been called in Christ, in the heavenly realms, far above all. They include practical guidance not only for individuals, but for husbands, wives, children and also for servants. The latter we could apply to those of us who serve others in employment. Such instruction will help us to put on the *new man* or Christ (Romans13:14) and walk in Him.

As I said earlier and repeat again, we do have a choice as Romans 6:13-14 implies by saying, "And do not present your members as instruments of unrighteousness to sin, but present yourselves to God as being alive from the dead, and your members as instruments of righteousness to God. For sin shall not have dominion over you, for you are not under law but under grace." Our body members can either be dominated for a while by the flesh, which can only lead to sin, or they can and should be dominated by the Spirit, which results in the fruits of righteousness. If we are genuine Christian believers, Christ is the ruler of our lives and the One who dominates us, not sin. Therefore lapses into sin should be temporary and not the mark of the true believer. Outbursts of anger, lying, unwholesome speech, or any other sin that is the trait of the *old man,* should not be the norm but rather considered out of character or untypical of those walking in Christ who are walking in love.

1 John 1:6-7 says, "If we say we have fellowship with Him, and walk in darkness, we lie and do not practise the truth. But if we walk in the light as He is in the light, we have fellowship with one another, and the blood of Jesus Christ His Son cleanses us from all sin." On the other hand, verse 8 continues, "If we say we have no sin, we deceive ourselves, and the truth is not in us."

Whilst we continue on our earthly journey we have no choice but to put up with the old nature, which is sinful. We must acknowledge this and be aware of it, but we must also keep it in check. But when it does raise its head and have its say, then 1 John 2:1-2 has some helpful words. "My little children, these things I write to you, that you may not sin. And if anyone sins, we have an Advocate with the Father, Jesus Christ the righteous. And He Himself is the propitiation for our sins, and not for ours only but also for the whole world."

Yes, Jesus Christ sits at the right hand of God as our Advocate. If we lapse into sin, then we can approach Him with sorrow in our hearts and confess, so that our fellowship with Him is not marred. Then we can continue to walk forward in the light and in joy of the new nature. Sin and the old nature are always associated with darkness, but we are light in the Lord (Ephesians 5:8-14). When we do sin the Holy Spirit, with whom we were sealed, is grieved and saddened and cannot work fully in our lives until we make our peace.

The old nature is under the control of Satan the devil. The following Bible verses hint at this being so:-

Ephesians 4:26-27: Be angry and do not sin, do not let the sun go down on your wrath, nor give place to the devil.

Ephesians 6:11: Put on the whole armour of God, that you may be able to stand against the wiles of the devil.

James 4:7: Therefore submit to God. Resist the devil and he will flee from you.

The devil is the prince, ruler or even god of this world (John 14:30; 2 Corinthians 4:4) and the whole world lies under his sway. That is why the Apostle John instructed us not to love the world or the things in it. Worldly desires are a distraction to our walk forward and Satan knows this. That is why he tries to spoil our walk by dangling things of this world in front of us—the things that the old nature loves. And if we bite, as we can do, then we allow him a foothold in our lives—that is until we come to our senses.

Satan knows that he can never undo or disqualify us from the work Christ has done on our behalf that gives us eternal life. He knows that he can never have full control of our lives anymore, but if he can temporarily disturb our peace then he will. Not that we can blame Satan for every wrong deed that we do. As we considered previously, it is out of the heart that wrong thoughts proceed which lead to sin. Even so, Satan has influenced men/women of God in the past to act wrongly. He tempted King David to number Israel instead of relying on God, and he filled the heart of Ananias and his wife so that they lied against the Holy Spirit.

Not only our actions but also our thinking can also be influenced by Satan through the old nature so that we come up with the wrong conclusion, as did the Apostle Peter when He confronted Jesus saying, "Far be it from You, Lord; this shall not happen to You." Christ rebuked Peter by saying to him, "Get behind Me Satan! You are an offence to Me, for you are not mindful of the things of God, but the things of men" (Matthew 16:22-23). On this particular occasion Peter's thoughts were being dominated by his old nature, under the control of the adversary, and were a spiritual hindrance to Christ and His way forward—hence Christ's strong rebuke.

Another point that I think is worthy of mention is good works. It is by the grace of God that we have been saved through faith (Ephesians 2:8). Verse 9 adds: "not of works, lest anyone should boast." Our salvation is not the result of any good works that we have done but based solely on the mercy of God. But verse 10 continues, "For we are His workmanship, created in Christ Jesus for good works, which God prepared beforehand that we should walk in them."

God has therefore prepared in advance good works in which He wishes us to partake and walk forward. Therefore, we need to take care that the good works that we do are those produced by following God's guidance in the Bible, and not of our own making to boost our pride.

Coming from a background of 'salvation by works' (that is before I really knew Christ as my Saviour), that is something I have experienced, and is a trait of the unconverted person, even if one is religious.

Before we move away from the subject of the activity of our body members, the Apostle James has much to say about one particular very small member and that is the tongue. He says this about it, "the tongue is a fire, a world of iniquity. The tongue is so set among our members so that it defiles the whole body."

Also, "no man can tame the tongue. It is an unruly evil, full of deadly poison. With it we bless our God and Father, and with it we curse men, who have been made in the similitude of God" (James 3:6,8-9).

How often have we allowed our tongue to get out of control and have said things that it was too late to take back? James acknowledges the way we are and that we all indeed do stumble in many things (v 2).

Yes, the old sinful nature and the new nature share the same tongue, so that out of the mouth proceed both blessings and cursings (v 10). Therefore, he encourages us to let our hearts be motivated by the wisdom from above, rather than by that which is earthly, sensual, even demonic.

The wisdom that comes from the new nature, which is from above, is pure, peaceable, gentle, willing to yield, full of mercy and good fruits and without hypocrisy (vs 13-18).

Conclusion

Conclusion

What practical measures then can we make to ensure that we walk forward worthily in the Spirit? Paul, in Romans 13:14, said that we are to make no provision for the flesh. In other words, we should not feed it with the things it loves, the things of this world, but rather starve it. He also said that we should put to death whatever belongs to our earthly nature. If we spend endless hours engaging in earthly pursuits, such as gaining material possessions, getting on in this world, watching worthless television, reading worldly books, newspapers or magazines, travelling, or pursuing earthly pleasures, at the expense of our spiritual life, then we are feeding the old nature. We are not storing treasures in heaven.

Whilst there are definitely many things of this world that are out of bounds to the Christian, and we don't need to spell out what these are, there is nothing wrong with some of the things mentioned above if they are pursued in moderation. It is when they crowd out the time we spend on spiritual things, like getting to know our Saviour better and gaining a better understanding of His will in the Bible and where we fit into it. These are the important things in life. All earthly pursuits are temporal but spiritual treasures are for an eternity (Matthew 6:19-21).

In the way that the physical body needs to be fed with the right kind of physical food and exercise if it is to be healthy, so it is with the spiritual being. It needs a regular diet of spiritual food from the word of God—His words are spirit, they are life! When we are feeding the new nature then we are starving the old. Whilst we might receive lots of spiritual benefit from food prepared for us by others, through church sermons, books etc., provided they are founded on the Word of God (2 Timothy 3:16-17), even so how much more nourishing to our spiritual life is it when we study the Bible ourselves, and do our own research into the word of God.

What joy it is to enjoy fellowship with God along with prayer and thanksgiving, as we unravel spiritual truths from His book of treasures, and then exercise them by making them part of our life and witness.

Another feature that will be helpful to us in our spiritual walk forward is to listen to our conscience. If it has been trained by the word of God, then it will give out the danger signs. When it begins to twinge it is for a reason and we should listen to it and take heed. We should never kid ourselves that we will always be okay and in full control. Watch for the danger signs and run in the opposite direction.

Finally

Finally

The aim of this booklet has been to help the reader rise above sin and its trappings, and "to walk in the Spirit". The fruit of God's Spirit is love. With this in mind Ephesians 5:2 tells us to 'walk in love', even as Christ also has loved us and given Himself for us. Christ and His sacrifice was the manifestation of God's love toward us (1 John 4:9-10). Therefore, Colossians 2:6 says,

> "As you have … received Christ Jesus the Lord, so walk in Him."

This we can do by submitting ourselves to Christ and allowing Him to work fully in our lives in and through the new nature. In Him we are complete (Colossians 2:10). He is the One who will enable us to reject all earthly desires and walk forward in the Spirit until we fulfil our earthly days.

By setting our heart and mind on things above, not on things of this earth, we are preparing ourselves for our future life with Christ, who is our life, and with whom our life is at present hidden. And when He appears we shall appear with Him in the glory (Colossians 3:1-4). On that day He will transform our lowly body that it may be conformed to His glorious body—a body that is compatible with our new nature (Philippians 3:21). Yes, our future is with Christ in the spiritual sphere, far above all, where we are to be blessed with every blessing that is spiritual, and our minds should be focussed on *Him*.

Those who are Christ's have crucified the flesh with its passions and desires.
If we live in the Spirit, let us also **WALK IN THE SPIRIT**
(Galatians 5:24-25)

The Work of the Spirit in an Age of Grace

By Michael Penny

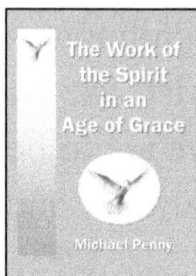

If you have enjoyed *To Walk in the Spirit* by Vicky Wilkinson, and would like to learn more about how the Spirit works in today's age of grace, then you will find *The Work of the Spirit in an Age of Grace* very helpful.

Within Christendom there is a wide variety of views on the work of the Holy Spirit. After Christ ascended into heaven, for the next thirty or so years, there was a profusion of overt action by the Spirit of God, but what after that? What do we discover in the letters written after the end of the Acts of the Apostles? What do they teach about the work of the Holy Spirit? This is what Michael Penny considers. Every reference to the 'Spirit' in the later letters is considered and commented upon. However, this book helps people come to their own understanding.

In part 1, each passage referring to the Spirit is quoted, followed by two or three questions for the reader to consider. In part 2 the author answers those questions and shares his understanding of what that passage shows is the work of the Holy Spirit as it relates to today's age of grace.

Great for personal study or group discussion.

Copies can also be ordered from
www.obt.org.uk

About the author

Vicky Wilkinson was born in Hull, East Yorkshire, in 1945 and was educated at Sidmouth High School and Hull College of Commerce. She worked as a shorthand typist before marrying and having four sons. She then returned to the workforce carrying out secretarial services for a local firm in Hull, where she lives with her husband and enjoys retirement.

Vicky Wilkinson was initially contacted by the Jehovah's Witnesses and was attracted to their position. However, through reading the Bible she came to see that salvation was by grace through faith in Jesus Christ, who was not 'a' God, but was 'the' God manifest in the flesh. She is a great advocate of the incarnation. Her story is told in her booklet *From Darkness to Glory*.

Also by Vicky Wilkinson

The Person of God in the Form of Man
Put on the Lord Jesus Christ
The Deity of Christ
What Christians believe and do
In Christ and with Christ
God's Work of Salvation
From Darkness to Glory
To walk in the Spirit

For further details of the above please visit

www.obt.org.uk/vicky-wilkinson

Free Magazine

Vicky Wilkinson is a regular contributor to
Search magazine

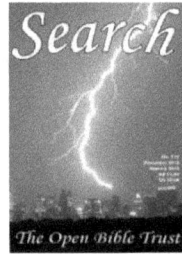

About this book

To Walk in the Spirit

The aim of this publication is to encourage, help and motivate Christians to rise above the temptation of the sin that is present in our permissive society, and "to walk in the Spirit", to display the "fruit the Spirit", and to "walk in love".

This we can do by setting our hearts and minds on things above, not on the things of this earth, and by submitting ourselves to Christ, and allowing Him to work fully in our lives, in and through our new nature. He is the One who can and will enable us to overcome earthly desires and "to walk in the Spirit".

As such, many Christians will find this booklet encouraging and helpful.

www.ingramcontent.com/pod-product-compliance
Lightning Source LLC
Chambersburg PA
CBHW070524030426
42337CB00016B/2101